BRIGHT IDEA BOOKS

YOU CAN WORK IN
Dance

by Samantha S. Bell

CAPSTONE PRESS
a capstone imprint

Bright Idea Books are published by Capstone Press
1710 Roe Crest Drive, North Mankato, Minnesota 56003
www.mycapstone.com

Library of Congress Cataloging-in-Publication Data
Names: Bell, Samantha, author.
Title: You can work in dance / By Samantha S. Bell.
Description: North Mankato, Minnesota : Capstone Press, [2019] | Series: You can work in the arts | Includes bibliographical references and index. | Audience: Grade 4 to 6.
Identifiers: LCCN 2018021289 (print) | LCCN 2018023378 (ebook) | ISBN 9781543541861 (ebook) | ISBN 9781543541465 (hardcover : alk. paper)
Subjects: LCSH: Dance--Vocational guidance--Juvenile literature.
Classification: LCC GV1596.5 (ebook) | LCC GV1596.5 .B45 2019 (print) | DDC 792.8023--dc23
LC record available at https://lccn.loc.gov/2018021289

Editorial Credits
Editor: Charly Haley
Designer: Becky Daum
Production Specialist: Claire Vanden Branden

Photo Credits
iStockphoto: DragonImages, 8–9, FilippoBacci, 24–25, gradyreese, 30–31, kzenon, 20, Mlenny, 6–7; Shutterstock Images, CREATISTA, 11, criben, 26–27, Diego Cervo, 15, Iakov Filimonov, 19, Igor Bulgarin, 12–13, Jacob Lund, 16–17, Nataliya Hora, 5, T-Design, cover (foreground), Tyler Olson, cover (background), wavebreakmedia, 23, 29

Design Elements: iStockphoto, Red Line Editorial, and Shutterstock Images

TABLE OF CONTENTS

CHAPTER 1

PROFESSIONAL
Dancers

The music starts. A dancer comes out onstage. She moves with the music. The dance may look smooth and easy. But it takes many hours of practice.

A ballet dancer performs set steps.

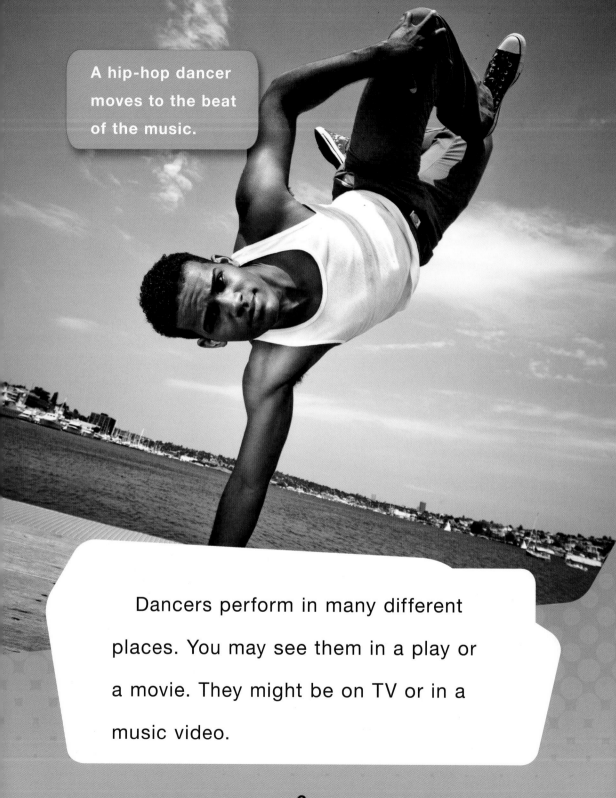

A hip-hop dancer moves to the beat of the music.

Dancers perform in many different places. You may see them in a play or a movie. They might be on TV or in a music video.

There are many styles of dance. Most dancers are good at one style. Some are **ballet** dancers. Some are **hip-hop** dancers. Some do **tap**, **salsa**, or **ballroom** dancing.

NEW MOVES

Some kinds of dance change over time. Hip-hop started in the 1970s. Dancers are still creating new moves.

Dancers practice as a group.

8

Dancers work very hard. They practice their **routines**.

A dancer must work well with others. Most dancers perform as a group. Some perform with a partner. They spend many hours together.

Most dancers start practicing when they are young. They take lessons from a dance teacher. Later they go to dance school.

CHAPTER 2

CHOREOGRAPHERS

Choreographers create dance routines. They decide the dance steps. Sometimes they choose the music and costumes.

Choreographers use dance to show a story or an idea. They make the movements fit the music. They make something new with each dance.

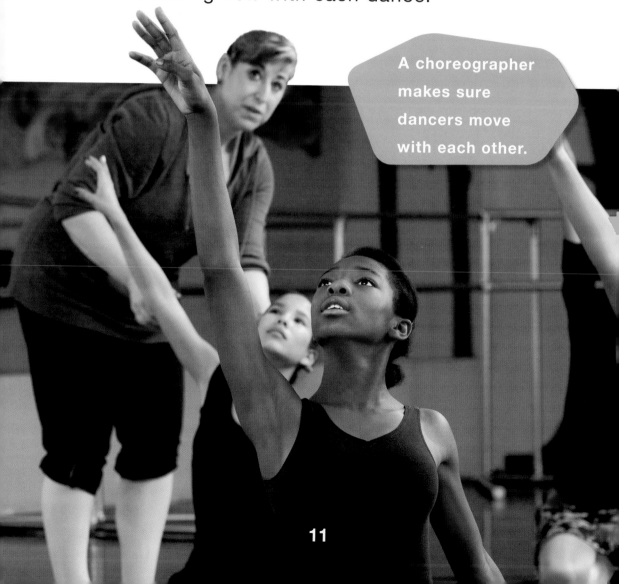

A choreographer makes sure dancers move with each other.

A choreographer creates dances for a musical.

Choreographers may work for dance companies. Dance companies have many dancers. Choreographers may work at schools or dance studios. They might work on **musicals**.

Choreographers must also be good teachers. They lead **rehearsals**. They show the dancers how to do the steps.

Some choreographers go to college. All start out as dancers. Some learn by creating dances for friends.

COSTUME DESIGNERS

Costume designers create the dance costumes. They work with choreographers. The costumes must fit the music and movement.

CHAPTER 3

ARTS
Managers

It takes more than just dancers to put on a performance. Someone needs to watch the dance. Arts **managers** bring dancers and audiences together.

Some managers work for dance companies. Others work in theaters. Some manage community projects.

An arts manager watches a dance rehearsal.

Managers work with the business side of dance. They plan events. They handle the money for events. They hire workers. They tell people to come to events.

Arts managers must be organized. They should be creative. Good managers love dance.

Some arts managers go to college. Some have dance training.

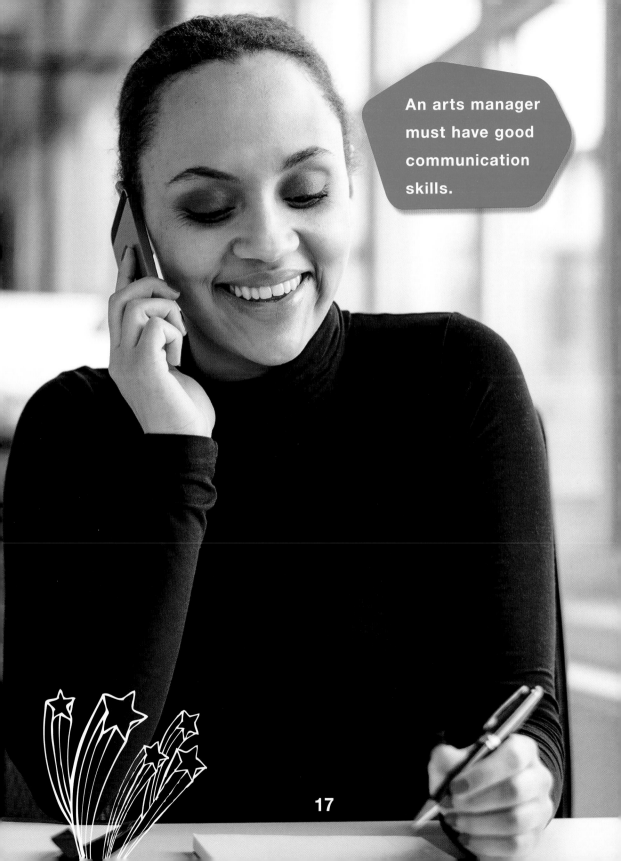

An arts manager must have good communication skills.

CHAPTER 4

DANCE
Teachers

Dance teachers show students how to practice. They teach them how to move safely. They teach them different types of dance.

Teachers decide the dance steps. They teach them to the students. The students perform the dances.

Some students dance for fun. Some want to work as dancers. Dance teachers help them reach their goals.

A dance teacher shows young students how to move.

A dance teacher may give
private lessons.

Dance teachers must be patient. They must work well with others. They must also be good leaders.

Some teach in a dance studio. They have danced a lot. Others teach in schools. They studied dance in college.

ON THEIR OWN

Some dance teachers have their own dance studio. They run it as a business.

CHAPTER 5

DANCE
Therapists

Dance **therapists** use dance to help others. They work with people of all ages.

Dance therapists want to help people feel good about themselves. They want people to feel **confident**. So they teach people to dance.

A dance therapist helps someone feel better through dance.

A dance therapist uses talking and dance to help someone deal with problems.

Dance therapists help people find ways to **cope** with problems. They help people deal with stress. They help people get along with others.

Some dance therapists work in schools. Others work in **counseling centers**. Some work in hospitals or nursing homes.

Dance therapists need to graduate from college. They also must know how to dance.

A dancer performs with musicians.

Some dancers perform. Some teach or help others. There are many different ways to work in dance!

GLOSSARY

ballet
a style of dance with set movements

ballroom
a style of dance for two people

choreographer
a person who makes dance routines

confident
believing in your abilities

cope
to deal with something difficult

counseling center
a place where people can get professional advice for personal problems

hip-hop
a fast-paced style of dance that started in African-American culture

manager
a person who is in charge of a project or organization

musical
a play on stage with songs and dancing

rehearsal
a time to practice before a performance

routine
a set of movements performed in a certain order

salsa
a Latin-American style of dance

tap
a dance performed in shoes that make tapping sounds

therapist
a person who professionally helps other people with their problems

FURTHER RESOURCES

Want to learn more about different styles of dance? Check out these resources:

Dancer.com: A list of ballet companies in the United States
https://dancer.com/ballet-info/online-resources/ballet-companies

Hill, Laban Carrick. *When the Beat Was Born: DJ Kool Herc and the Creation of Hip Hop*. New York: Roaring Brook Press, 2013.

PBS: The Funky Business of Kids' Competitive Break Dancing
https://www.pbs.org/newshour/show/the-funky-business-of-kids-competitive-break-dancing

How can you start working in dance? Check out this book to learn more:

Van der Linde, Laurel. *So You Want to Be a Dancer? The Ultimate Guide to Exploring the Dance Industry*. Hillsboro, Ore.: Beyond Words, 2015.

Do you just want to learn more about dancing? Check out these websites:

Dance Magazine
http://www.dancemagazine.com

PBS: What's Good: Dance
http://www.pbs.org/video/dance-kxhuco

ACTIVITY

CREATE YOUR OWN DANCE ROUTINE!

Choose a song. Now create a dance to go with the song. Think about how the words and music make you feel. Create your own dance moves to express those feelings. Perform your dance for family or friends. You can even teach them your new dance routine!

INDEX